FIGHTING FOR EQUALITY: A BRIEF HISTORY OF AFRICAN AMERICANS IN AMERICA

United States 1877-1914

American World History | History 6th Grade | Children's American History of 1800s

BABY PROFESSOR
EDUCATION KIDS

First Edition, 2020

Published in the United States by Speedy Publishing LLC, 40 E Main Street, Newark, Delaware 19711 USA.

© 2020 Baby Professor Books, an imprint of Speedy Publishing LLC

Baby Professor Books are available at special discounts when purchased in bulk for industrial and sales-promotional use. For details contact our Special Sales Team at Speedy Publishing LLC, 40 E Main Street, Newark, Delaware 19711 USA. Telephone (888) 248-4521 Fax: (210) 519-4043.

10 9 8 7 6 * 5 4 3 2 1

Print Edition: 9781541950498
Digital Edition: 9781541952294
Hardcover Edition: 9781541976641

See the world in pictures. Build your knowledge in style.
www.speedypublishing.com

TABLE OF CONTENTS

In this book, we're going to talk about the history of African Americans in the United States from 1877 to 1914, so let's get right to it!

When Did Africans Come to North America?

At the beginning of the 17th century, the colonists in North America took in poor Europeans to help them meet their needs for labor. These Europeans were indentured servants. Once they labored for a certain amount of time to pay off their debts they became free from their employers. They were servants, but they were not slaves.

COLONIAL AMERICAN PLUMBER AND DYER ASSISTED BY INDENTURED SERVANTS.

However, as the colonies continued to grow, the need for men and women to perform manual labor continued to increase and there weren't enough laborers to fill the need. The wealthy landowners began to seek out less expensive sources for labor and that's when the slave trade began.

SLAVE TRADE BEGAN WHEN WEALTHY LANDOWNERS BEGAN TO SEEK OUT LESS EXPENSIVE SOURCES FOR LABOR.

In 1619, about 20 Africans were brought to the colonies by a Dutch ship. When they arrived at the city of Jamestown in the colony of Virgina, they were purchased by some of the colonists. The era of slave labor in the colonies began. Today it's difficult to think of human beings being bought and sold, but that's what enslavement means. For the most part, the slaves did what their masters told them to do, morning, noon, and night.

THE ARRIVAL OF 20 AFRICAN CAPTIVES AT JAMESTOWN FROM DUTCH MAN-OF-WAR IN 1619.

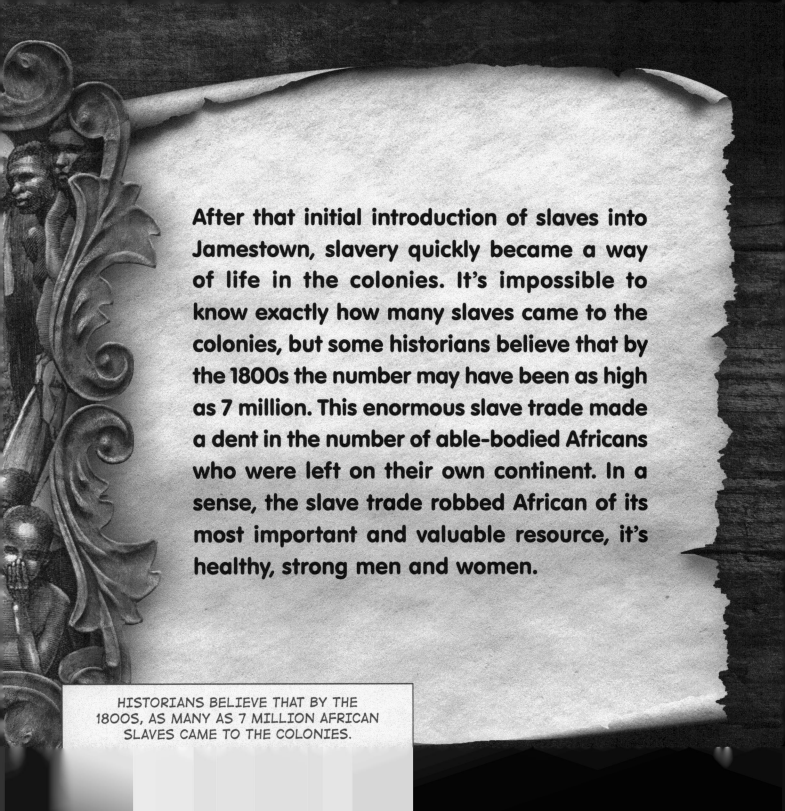

After that initial introduction of slaves into Jamestown, slavery quickly became a way of life in the colonies. It's impossible to know exactly how many slaves came to the colonies, but some historians believe that by the 1800s the number may have been as high as 7 million. This enormous slave trade made a dent in the number of able-bodied Africans who were left on their own continent. In a sense, the slave trade robbed African of its most important and valuable resource, it's healthy, strong men and women.

HISTORIANS BELIEVE THAT BY THE 1800S, AS MANY AS 7 MILLION AFRICAN SLAVES CAME TO THE COLONIES.

A Shift in Attitude

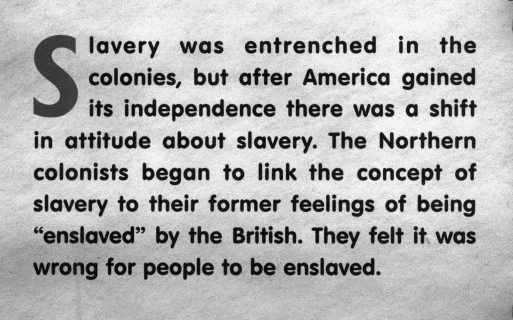

Slavery was entrenched in the colonies, but after America gained its independence there was a shift in attitude about slavery. The Northern colonists began to link the concept of slavery to their former feelings of being "enslaved" by the British. They felt it was wrong for people to be enslaved.

THE NORTHERN COLONISTS FELT IT WAS
WRONG FOR PEOPLE TO BE ENSLAVED.

However, in the South, slave labor was important because the plantations could not survive without the inexpensive labor of slaves. So, the colonists in the South remained entrenched and wouldn't shift their thinking regarding slaves.

IN THE SOUTH, SLAVE LABOR WAS IMPORTANT BECAUSE THE PLANTATIONS COULD NOT SURVIVE WITHOUT THE INEXPENSIVE LABOR OF SLAVES.

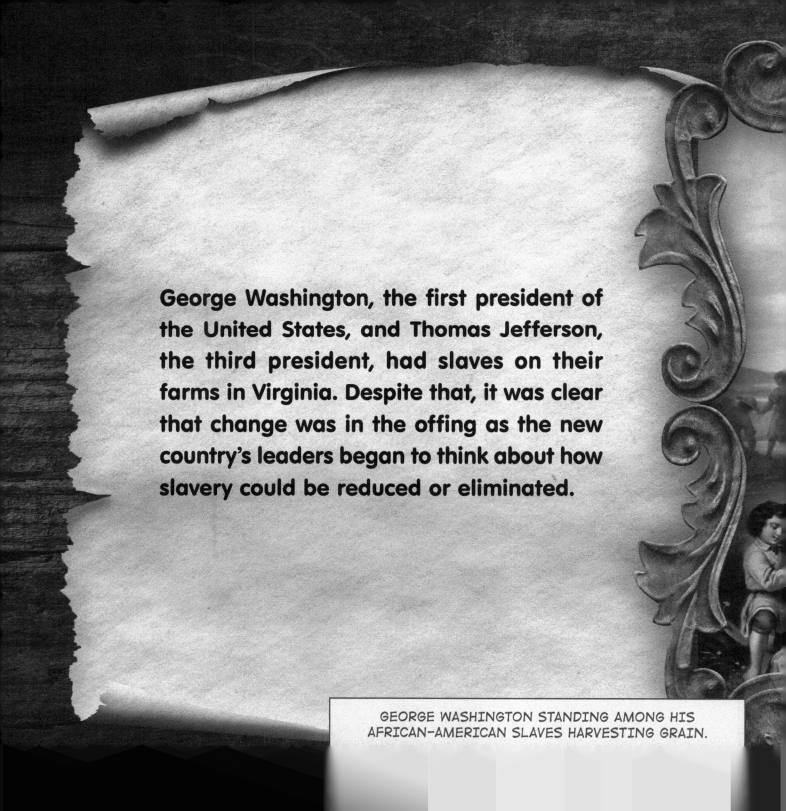

George Washington, the first president of the United States, and Thomas Jefferson, the third president, had slaves on their farms in Virginia. Despite that, it was clear that change was in the offing as the new country's leaders began to think about how slavery could be reduced or eliminated.

GEORGE WASHINGTON STANDING AMONG HIS AFRICAN-AMERICAN SLAVES HARVESTING GRAIN.

After all, the United States was a country founded on freedom, so it seemed unjust that some people, namely the African Americans, didn't have the freedom to do what they wanted to do or live the way they wanted to live. At that time, even the Constitution gave people the right to buy "persons held for labor and service," which was a euphemism for the condition of slavery.

Toward the final part of the 18th century, slavery was a vital part of plantation life in the south. The economy there was dependent on cotton and tobacco. Even though Congress had passed a law in 1808 stating that the buying and selling of slaves was officially outlawed, the population of slaves continued to increase. By the year 1860, there were over 4 million slaves living and working in the colonies. Over 50% of the slave population was supporting the cotton-producing regions of the South.

SLAVES PICKING COTTON IN THE SOUTH.

The Cotton Industry in 1793

After the Revolutionary War, the South was challenged by economic uncertainty. At one time the soil was fertile for supporting tobacco, but it soon became depleted. The landowners tried to plant rice as well as indigo, but these crops didn't make enough profit. In the midst of this turmoil, the textile industry began to boom in England. Cotton was needed to make these textiles and cotton had been grown successfully in the South. But as demand for cotton increased, the plantations couldn't keep up because of one simple fact—it was incredibly difficult to extract the seeds from the cotton fibers. This process had to done by hand and it was very laborious.

A COTTON PLANTATION ON THE MISSISSIPPI RIVER WITH AFRICAN AMERICAN WORKERS.

Then in 1793 everything changed when an inventor by the name of Eli Whitney solved the problem. He invented the cotton gin, a machine designed to extract the seeds. Within a few short years, the South had transitioned from the main crop of tobacco to the main crop of cotton and the need for slave labor was higher than ever.

ELI WHITNEY

SLAVES USING ELI WHITNEY'S COTTON GIN.

After the Civil War

Six decades of slave labor passed by before the issue of slavery caused a major schism in the country. Northerners wanted to abolish slavery and southerners wanted to keep it. This issue was the major cause of the Civil War, which lasted from 1861 to 1865.

UNION AND CONFEDERATE TROOPS DURING THE CIVIL WAR.

After the South lost and the Reconstruction period began, the Constitution was amended to officially abolish slavery. A series of amendments were passed.

The 13th Amendment was added in 1865 and stated that slavery should be abolished.

The 14th Amendment was added in 1868 and stated that former slaves should have equal protection under the law.

JOINT HOUSE AND SENATE RECONSTRUCTION COMMITTEE CREATING 14TH AMENDMENT UNDER CHAIRMAN WILLIAM FESSENDEN.

CITIZENS CHEERING
OUTSIDE THE CAPITOL AS
THE US CONGRESS PASSES
THE 14TH AMENDMENT

AFRICAN AMERICAN ELECTION OFFICIAL SUPERVISING THE FIRST BLACK VOTERS IN WASHINGTON, DC

The 15th Amendment was added in 1870 and stated that African Americans could now vote and be elected to public office.

THE FIFTEENTH AMENDMENT.

A PRINT ILLUSTRATING THE RIGHTS GRANTED BY THE 15TH AMENDMENT.

As African Americans began to exercise their rights, many people in the South could not accept it. Secret societies of white supremacists, such as the Ku Klux Klan, known as the KKK, used violence and intimidation to sabotage the African Americans' newfound freedom and power.

A CEREMONY OF THE KU KLUX KLAN.

By 1877, as the Reconstruction period began to end, the last soldiers departed from the area. Although laws supposedly protected them, the former slaves had not gained the equal status they wished for. Their gains toward equality had been destroyed by the KKK.

KU KLUX KLAN MEMBERS SHOOTING AN AFRICAN-AMERICAN FAMILY IN THEIR CABIN IN THE SOUTH.

Separate But Equal

Northerners who had moved to the South to free the slaves were called carpetbaggers because they carried their possessions in cheap sacks. They were perceived by southerners to be unscrupulous opportunists.

CARPETBAGGERS ARE NORTHERNERS WHO HAD MOVED TO THE SOUTH TO FREE THE SLAVES.

Once they began to leave, the southerners started to pass laws to segregate black people from white people again. These laws were called "Jim Crow" laws. The term "Jim Crow" was used as a derogatory term for African Americans. It was based on a minstrel performance where a white actor put on a blackface.

THOMAS "DADDY" RICE WAS A WHITE PERFORMER WHO USED AFRO-AMERICAN SPEECH WHILE DANCING AS A MINSTREL TO CREATE "JIM CROW".

These segregation laws kept African Americans in separate schools, separate seating in public transportation, and separate facilities in hotels, restaurants, and theaters.

A SEGREGATED SCHOOL FOR AFRICAN AMERICANS IN NEW YORK CITY.

Then, in 1896, there was a famous court case that got taken up to the Supreme Court. The case was Plessy versus Ferguson. It was the first case that tested the strength of the 14th Amendment. There was a law in Louisiana that forced African Americans to sit in different railroad cars away from the white passengers. Instead of saying this law violated the amendment, the Supreme Court ruled that if the accommodations were equivalent then it met the requirements of the amendment. In other words, it was okay to segregate African Americans as long as the conditions were "separate but equal."

A FREEMAN BEING EXPELLED BY THE CONDUCTOR OF A RAILROAD CAR.

For 58 years, this case was used to assess whether segregation laws were in violation of the Constitution. Finally, in 1954, it was reversed by another famous court case, which was Brown versus Board of Education.

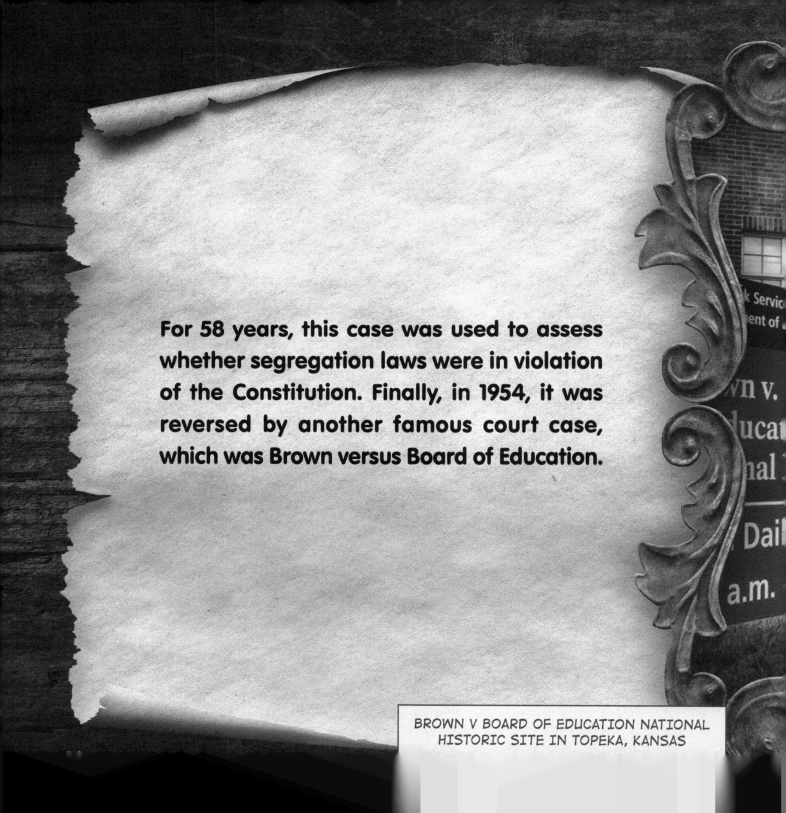

BROWN V BOARD OF EDUCATION NATIONAL HISTORIC SITE IN TOPEKA, KANSAS

Booker T. Washington, George Washington Carver, and Du Bois

In the South, at the end of the 19th century, segregation had a more forceful stronghold than ever before. Frustrated with their lack of progress toward true equality, African Americans began to look at education as a way out of their plight. The famous African American author and educator, Booker T. Washington, was an inspiration with his book called *Up From Slavery*. He encouraged black people to gain skills to ensure their security in the rapidly evolving job market.

COVER OF THE FIRST EDITION OF UP FROM SLAVERY, THE AUTOBIOGRAPHY OF BOOKER T. WASHINGTON.

UP FROM SLAVERY
AN AUTOBIOGRAPHY
BOOKER T. WASHINGTON

BOOKER T. WASHINGTON

GEORGE WASHINGTON
CARVER

Another former slave, George Washington Carver, was an inspiration as well. A scientist and inventor, he persuaded farmers in the south to plant peanuts and soybeans to replenish the soil.

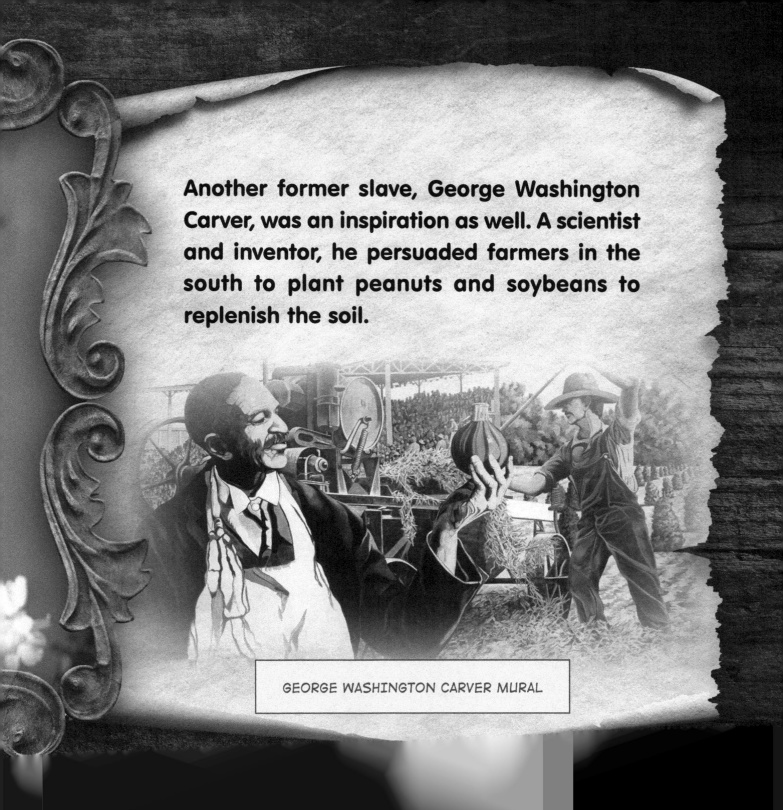

GEORGE WASHINGTON CARVER MURAL

W.E.B. DU BOIS

During the first part of the 20th century, W.E.B. Du Bois, a Harvard educated sociologist, became a leading voice for protests. His book, *Souls of Black Folk,* took the position that African Americans should strive for higher education.

The Founding of the NAACP

In 1905, Du Bois started an organization. The members convened at Niagara Falls on the Canadian side and thus their activities were called the Niagara Movement. At this time in history, there were problems with employment and also with housing.

FOUNDERS OF THE NIAGARA MOVEMENT IN 1905. DU BOIS IS IN THE MIDDLE ROW, WITH WHITE HAT.

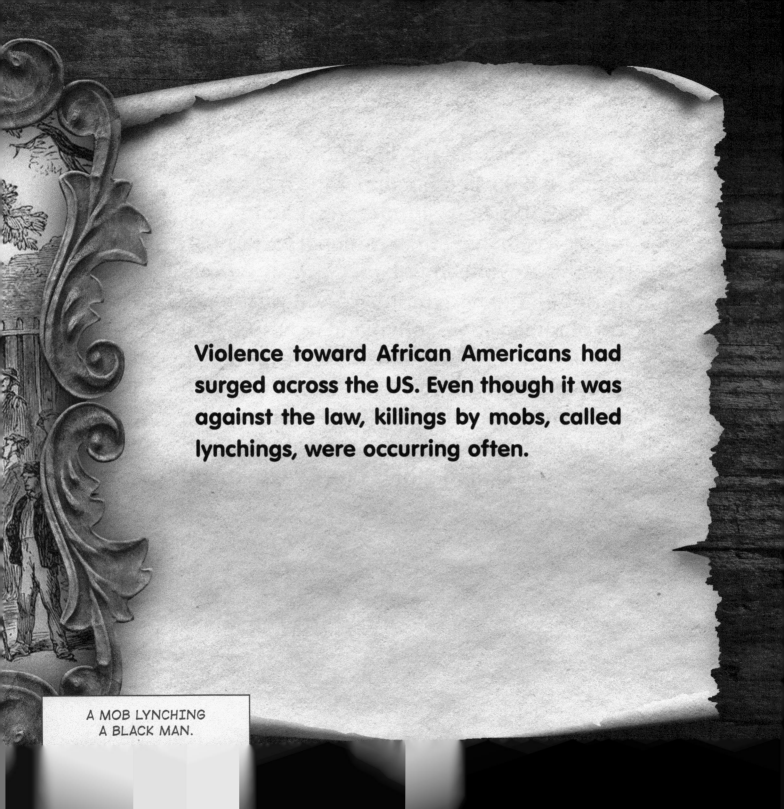

Violence toward African Americans had surged across the US. Even though it was against the law, killings by mobs, called lynchings, were occurring often.

A MOB LYNCHING A BLACK MAN.

A significant race riot in Illinois, which took place in 1908, lit a fire under the movement. In 1909, Du Bois' supporters joined their mission with that of the National Association for the Advancement of Colored People (NAACP). The goal of the NAACP was to get rid of forced segregation and to ensure that the 14th and 15th Amendments were enforced. They also sought to have equal education for African Americans. NAACP (read as the N-double A-CP) began to establish itself across the United States and by 1921 it had over 400 locations.

NAACP LOGO

AN ILLUSTRATION DEPICTING A RACE RIOT.

Summary

The first Africans who came to the colonies were slaves. The colonists needed slave labor to do the lion's share of the work. The Civil War broke out in 1861. When the war was over in 1865, the Constitution was amended to show that slavery had been abolished. However, the South retained its old ways and continued to pass segregation laws.

The Supreme Court stated that "separate, but equal" facilities were acceptable, which was a blow to African Americans. It wasn't until 1954 that another case overturned the "separate but equal" way of viewing the amendments. During this pivotal time from 1877 to 1914, African Americans made progress in their long battle to become free of prejudice and claim their birthright to equality.

Awesome! Now that you've learned about the history of African Americans from pre-1877 to 1914, you may want to read about African Americans during the 1960s in the Baby Professor Book, *C is for Civil Rights Books: The African American Civil Rights Movement | Children's History Books.*

Lightning Source UK Ltd.
Milton Keynes UK
UKHW050751050121
376449UK00002B/78